THE CREDIT RESET

A MODERN GUIDE TO REPAIRING YOUR CREDIT

VERNELL WATTS

outskirts
press

Due to the Abundance of conflicting information about credit, it can be difficult to understand what works and what doesn't. In this book, I will lay out the exact steps you must take to improve your credit and achieve homeownership.

This book will not only break down the intricacies of credit, but it will also act as a step by step guide on disputing negative accounts. Potential clients often ask me if they could repair their credit on their own; my answer is always the same... OF COURSE. You could improve your credit on your own just like you can represent yourself in court, sell a house without a realtor, do your car repairs, etc. Still, some insist on doing it themselves; this is why I wrote this book. If you are going to go at this with no professional help, there is nothing more important than having a proven formula at your disposal.

Table of Contents

About My Company and Me

BEFORE WE GET into any credit repair, I would like to introduce myself. My name is Vernell Watts, and I am the founder of Fortune 800. Fortune 800 is a results-driven Credit improvement and homeownership preparation company. Our focus is to help potential homeowners prepare for what will likely be the largest purchase they'll make in their lifetime.

If you are skeptical about the information and asking yourself, "will this help me?" I understand. A lot of companies give false grantees and sell false promises. My company is all about transparency and honesty. This process is not easy. With that said, I will not make you any guarantees. Instead, I will show you the blueprint and let you experience the results that these strategies yield. You can also go to fortune800.com/success and look at our success stories.

How It Started

Right out of high school, I decided to get my real estate license; after I finished my testing and got my license, my mom told me one of her friends was in credit repair and wanted us to join. In my head, I was thinking, "Credit repair and Real estate go hand and hand," I told her I wanted to get in on it.

Here's how the company operated; once you paid the "startup fee" of nearly $300, now could promote the company's service. You could also recruit people to sell the service and make money that way as well. Most people would refer to this as a pyramid scheme, MLM or, network marketing. I started promoting the service and made some money through direct sales and recruiting; at this point, I decided to go all-in on credit repair and promote this service.

After a few months, I realized I was getting 100% negative feedback from clients. People were being sued, and NO ONE was getting any results. The biggest red flag is when one of my mom clients called her, and she said, "I got my letters in today, and I am getting ready send them, but the letters say this is not my account, the account is mine though" She replied 'The company has a lot of experience and knows what they are doing, I am sure you'll be fine if you send the letters" We will cover why sending letters like this is a mistake later in the book.

After this, another one of our clients, a close family member, called us and told us she was being sued by a finance company that financed her car 15 years ago. She had just got a new job with a drastic pay raise and was having her wages garnished. At this point, I knew there was no way I could continue to promote this company. The worst part is I didn't have answers for anyone; I didn't know why all this was happening; I thought I was helping them.

By now, you can understand why it can be destructive to have someone who doesn't understand the laws of credit repair, promoting services as if they do. After all, that went down; I decided I would study the law and learn the ins and outs of credit so I can find out what happened. After I put the pieces together, I realized not only did I need to spread this information, I needed to offer an alternative service that was far superior to what was already out there. That is when I decided to start my own company, and Fortune 800 was born.

That is enough about me and my story; time to get into the blueprint to achieving good credit and homeownership.

"Your credit can be your largest asset or your largest liability."

CHAPTER 1

What is credit...

Understanding the basics

CREDIT IS JUST the ability to consume goods and or services now with the intention the consumer will be able to pay back later. Have you ever lent a friend or family money for food because they forgot their wallet or for some emergency? You gave them credit; they get whatever it is they needed now and pay you back for it later. Now let me ask you this if you lent out money, and the person did not pay you back on the terms you agreed upon, how likely is it that you will lend them money again? I am guessing not very likely, and this is the exact situation most people are in. They got approved for some form of credit, was able to obtain some form of goods or services, and didn't pay as agreed, therefore ruining their creditability, making them impossible to lend to.

Now, what could a person in a situation like this do? The obvious answer is to pay as agreed, but we all know that when something is easy to do, it just as easy not to do, and things happen. You can restore your good name and take control of your credit score, but to do this, you must understand how credit works.

Understanding your score

Show me and 800 credit score and I show you someone who understands how credit works.

Here's a break of how exactly your credit score is calculated and how to maximize each category. Once you know the basics, you can start to control your credit score rather than it controlling you.

- **35% Payment history** This obvious PAY YOUR BILLS, but this is not always this simple. To avoid this, set up automatic payments if you can't seem to pay your bills, but I set up payment date notifications and transaction notifications. If you have late payments, we will talk about how to get those removed as well.
- **30% Utilization** Utilization is the amount borrowed vs. the amount available to borrow. If you have a card with a $1,000 limit and use $300, your utilization is 30%. This is why when someone maxes out a card, their score can drop anywhere from 20-45 points depending on your score. A Great Tool you can use to prevent this is a balance notification. The Credit card company will notify you once you have spent a certain amount on your credit. You can choose what amount.
- **15% Age of Accounts** This 15% part of your score is why someone with a new credit profile cannot have perfect credit. The bureaus average out the age of your accounts, and more age equals more credibility.

Often consumers close their credit cards after paying it down just so they never have to deal with the card. This is never a good idea, especially if the account is reporting positively. If you really cannot help but use your card, here is my advice to you, use the card to pay some monthly subscription you were going to pay for anyway, cut the card up and continue to pay the bill through the bank's mobile banking app. Closing accounts in good standing will not only affect the age of accounts but will also affect your utilization rate since the amount of credit available to you will be lowered, making your utilization rate higher.

- **10% Credit Mix** The credit bureaus consider your mix between the three types of credit accounts when calculating your score. Those accounts are **Open accounts,** accounts that need to be paid in full at the end of every month. **Revolving accounts,** an account with no set payment and can be used to borrow against over and over. **Installment accounts,** accounts that have set monthly payments. 99.9% of the time, this is not where people go wrong when it comes to their credit, but it is something to consider when applying for new accounts.

- **10% New Credit and Inquiries** Excessive inquiries in a short time will not only lower your score but will have you automatically denied by most bank underwriting systems when applying for new credit. As mentioned earlier, credit is for people who don't need it, so when you apply for credit excessively, you will appear desperate to the creditors. Inquiries will have a small impact on your score for 24 months, and after that time, they will not affect your score.

The 30% trap

If you have ever read another book on credit or watched a YouTube video about credit, you have probably heard the advice "Keep your utilization just under 30%". The 30 percent rule will not move the needle if you want to see drastic changes in your score. Rather the 3% rule will give you the results that get you approved for that dream home or that dream car. The 3% means you are only using 3% of your available credit so, take each line of credit you have available and multiply it by .03. Once you can achieve using the debt elimination strategies, your score will not only increase drastically, but it will keep you motivated, moving forward to conquer this journey.

You may be asking yourself: "why is 3% the magic number?" and I would say because this number represents that your accounts are actively being used but at the same time are not being overused. If your accounts are overused, the bureaus will take it; you're an irresponsible borrower, and if they are underused, the credit bureaus will see you as someone not actively using your accounts; both will hurt your score.

Credit Card utilization is the elephant in the room and the reason why most people have low scores. You can remove anything you want off of your credit score, whether it be collection accounts, bankruptcies, or public records, but if you have three maxed out credit cards, your score will suffer.

**"The less you need credit,
the more of it you can get"**

CHAPTER 2

How credit reporting works...

Why your scores are different

WHEN YOU HAVE an open line of credit with a company, that company can choose whether or not they want to report your activity on that account to the credit bureaus or not. While big-name creditors such as American Express or Discover report to the credit bureaus smaller name creditors such as your local buy here pay here car lots or your no credit check furniture stores can pick and choose what bureaus they report to. They can also choose whether or not they report at all, and this is one of the reasons reason why you have different scores. Your car loan may be reporting on Experian and Equifax, but nothing on Transunion or you may have two negatively reporting accounts on Transunion and Equifax, but it doesn't show up on Experian.

I had a falsely reporting account on Experian that had a 170-day late payment, and it made my score a 650 while I had 727 Equifax and 737 Transunion. Some statistics say 1 out

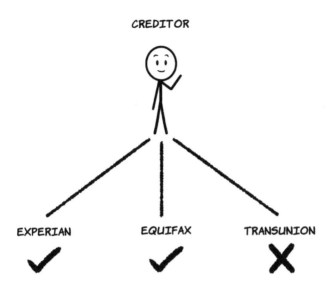

of 5 credit reports have errors, and some statistics say 1 out of 7, but my question is who is tracking these statistics and how they would come up with the statistics unless they intended to report errors. Whether or not they are reporting mistakes on purpose or not, the credit bureaus don't have enough manpower to verify every account for every report. That is why there is an opportunity to repair your credit.

Scores Vs. Reports

During the credit repair process, you have to ignore the score and pay close attention to the report. Your score is important, but I remember having a 717 credit score and applying for my 3rd card with Chase, and I thought I would be approved instantly since my score was 717, but I ended up getting denied. Once I got the letter from Chase in the mail with the reason I was rejected, the reason was lack of established accounts; this is when I realized that although the FICO score is important, it is not the end all be all. The information that is inside of your credit report is what garners you your credibility, not the score itself.

It is not hard to have a useless 700 credit score using authorized user tradelines. Authorized user tradelines are how I jumpstarted my credit score. Authorized user tradelines are just rented credit history from someone else's account that can be applied to yours; we'll go into detail on this later on. To restore your good name, we must ignore the scores and focus on what makes you credible, which is the information inside your credit report.

FICO VS FAKO

Commonly, someone will check their Credit Karma account, and their score seems as if it is decent, maybe a 660-680 is the score that pops up. This person sees that they have decent credit, and they head out to the car dealership. This person arrives, and the dealership runs their credit score and Boom, 619. When it comes to credit monitoring services, I believe they are great for monthly or weekly updates and to get a ballpark of where your score lyes, but it doesn't capture and show you your real score. The scores you see on credit monitoring services are not FICO scores but Vantage 3.0 scores, and it is calculated differently. Here's how Vantage Score 3.0 is calculated...

Payment History 40%

This scoring model gives you an extra 5% toward payment history compared to the 35% you get for payment history in the traditional scoring model. If you do a great job when it comes to paying your bills on time, but you carry high balances on your credit cards, and you have low limits when you go in check your FICO score, it can be significantly different from what you might see on credit karma or any credit monitoring service.

Age and type of credit 21%

This factor refers to how long you have had different types of accounts open. We talked about the different accounts being Revolving, Installment, and open accounts. As long as you have various accounts and you don't have a bunch of late payments on each one, you are in good shape.

Credit utilization 20%

When you carry high balances and have low limits, you will be viewed as irresponsible, which applies to any scoring model. We will go over how to increase your credit card limits later in the book.

Balances 11%

This section focuses on your recent balances on your accounts. Keep low balances on your cards with low limits.

Recent Credit 5%

Opening new accounts will change how lenders will look at your future financial performance based on how often you open new accounts

Available credit 3%

If you have high credit card limits and use them responsibly, you will be rewarded.

This is just one of many different scores that are used; here is a list of all the current scoring models.

28 FICO SCORES

EQUIFAX	EXPERIAN	TRANSUNION
• FICO 8	• FICO 8	• FICO SCORE 8
• FICO MORT. SCORE 5*	• FICO MORT. SCORE 2*	• FICO MORT, SCORE 4*
• FICO AUTO SCORE 5	• FICO AUTO SCORE 2	• FICO AUTO SCORE 4
• FICO AUTO SCORE 8	• FICO AUTO SCORE 8	• FICO AUTO SCORE 8
• FICO AUTO SCORE 9	• FICO AUTO SCORE 9	• FICO AUTO SCORE 9
• FICO BANKCARD 8	• FICO BANKCARD 8	• FICO BANKCARD 8
• FICO BANKCARD 5	• FICO BANKCARD 2	• FICO BANKCARD 4
• FICO BANKCARD 9	• FICO SCORE 3	• FICO BANKCARD 9
• FICO SCORE 9	• FICO BANKCARD 9	• FICO SCORE 9
	• FICO SCORE 9	

10 Reasons To Have Good Credit

Some people have destroyed their credit due to an unpaid cable bill and a $500 credit card and have learned to live with bad credit. Living with bad credit is possible, but why financially cripple yourself when it could have easily been avoided by reading a few books and applying what you read?

Most people are not walking around with bags of cash waiting to pay for their homes. If you don't plan on owning either of these, you still need a place to live, and don't worry; there are credit checks for renters as well

People with bad credit get nickel and dimed. You will be charged every fee possible, be faced with having to pay high deposits, and pay ridiculously high-interest rates. If you walk into any financial establishment that is willing to lend to people with bad credit, whoever is there assisting you will be happy to attach a 19% APR to your loan and will do so with a big smile on their face. Being ignorant will cost you thousands over your lifetime. Do you think it is just a coincidence that payday loans, title loans, and check cashing centers infest the lower-income areas? Credit is designed to benefit those who understand it and prey on those who don't, and fortunately, you can pick which side you want to be on.

If you run into someone who has given up on their credit, they might try to convince you why credit is bad or why you shouldn't use credit. You and I both know that there are ZERO benefits to having bad credit. With that said, here are ten reasons you should have a good credit score

10 Reasons to have good credit
1. To Own a house to build equity and avoid rising rents
2. To Secure Funds for a business
3. To qualify for the best insurance premium
4. To be hired a job that checks your score
5. Finance a car at a reasonable rate
6. Access To rewards credit cards (Travel, Cash Back)
7. Have Accesses to credit in case an emergency
8. Low deposits for leases
9. Borrow low-interest loans for college
10. Zero Liability rental car insurance

"To win the game, you must understand the rules."

CHAPTER 3

The FICO Scare

EVERY FIVE YEARS, FICO releases a new fico scoring model, and consumers get nervous. Propaganda floods the internet about how everyone's FICO score will go from 800 to 200 overnight, but these "experts" or whoever is covering the topic fails to mention one important thing...

Lenders get to choose which fico score they use. We are currently on FICO 10, but many lenders still use the FICO 8 scoring model. Though this is true, let's cover the fico 10 scoring model anyway...

According to Experian, "FICO®, has built a new suite of scoring models that will be available from all three credit reporting agencies (Experian, TransUnion, and Equifax) to lenders by the end of 2020. The new models will treat late payments and debt more severely, but will also now consider historical information about your credit card balances and payment amounts. Your FICO® Score will likely change as a result." All this means is if you have a lot of debt, your score will suffer even more.

Since you are reading this, I will put you ahead of the

curve and show you how to lower your debts and improve your credit strategically.

Although it is essential to know how your credit score works and how it's calculated, it is equally as important to understand who is housing this information. Here are all the entities that house our information

Original Creditor The original creditors are the ones who extended us credit lines—companies such as credit card companies, credit unions, finance companies, car dealerships, etc. If you pay these companies on time and avoid opening many accounts, you will be fine.

Credit Bureaus The credit bureaus are just a data source. They do not determine whether you are approved or denied; they only provide the data. These companies make their money by selling our information to original creditors. This is the reason you Get pre approvals in the mail.

Credit Reporting Agency A credit reporting agency is a little different than a credit bureau. The rules and regulations they follow are slightly different. Reporting agencies house precise information about us. Information such as banking history, income, legal information, etc.

Collection Agencies If you cannot pay back your original Creditor, they will sell the debt to a collection agency. Collection agencies buy debt from original creditors in bulk and collect on it for a profit. Dealing with collection agencies can be a slippery slope; we'll break down how to deal with collections later in the book.

The Role they play

These large companies that determine how easy or difficult someone's life will be, such as Experian, Equifax, and Transunion, are not government agencies, and there is no reason to be afraid of them. They store and report your financial habits, put it into an algorithm, and boom, either you're paying 4% interest on that new car loan or paying 13%. These companies make mistakes and aren't held accountable. Databases have been breached and identities compromised because of these companies, and you are telling me I should just trust these companies and just patiently wait seven years for an account to fall off that might not even be reporting accurately? Yeah right. Here is a summary of each credit bureau and its role in housing your information.

Experian

Experian houses both consumer and business credit files. The information of 235 million consumers is held with Experian. Experian uses this data to offer their other services, such as decision analytics and business marketing consulting.

Equifax

Equifax also houses consumer and business credit files of 800 million consumers and 89 million businesses worldwide. Equifax is known for false and outdated information and receives the bulk of complaints from consumers.

Transunion

This Credit Bureau is the smallest of the three bureaus and houses upwards of 200 million consumer credit reports in the United States.

"Large corporations are not your friends."

CHAPTER **4**

Who is telling you?

WHILE THERE ARE the three major credit bureaus, Experian, Equifax and Transunion are the largest companies that house our information. We call them the roleplayers; these companies play a role when it comes to getting you approved for that brand new car down to get a collection account removed off of your credit report. The three big roleplayers that help the bureaus verify your negative accounts are...

Lexis Nexus

Lexis Nexus is a private entity with one of the world's largest databases. Lexis Nexus houses and resell our legal and public record information and act as a middle man between the CourtHouses and Record Recorders and The large credit bureaus; Equifax, Transunion, and Experian. The Courthouses and Record Recorders are not allowed to feed information to the credit bureaus; this is why Lexis Nexus Plays a big role in verifying accounts such as public records and bankruptcy. This Is how the flow of information works...

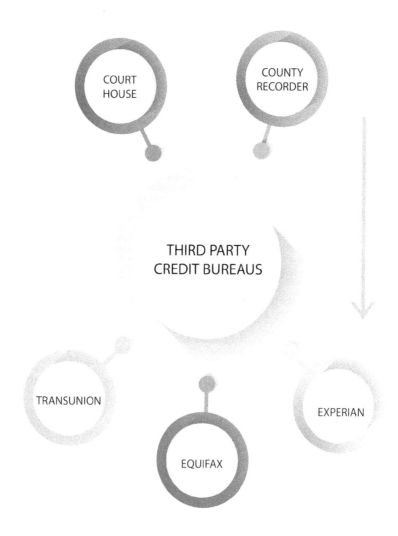

Innovis

This lesser-known credit bureau focuses on fraud protection and prevention. You check your report with this company for free once a year.

Sage stream

Sage Stream focuses on consumers age 18-34 specifically. Around these ages, people have less credit activity. In many cases, individuals the age of 18-27, there is no credit activity for many members of this group. According to Sage Stream LLC's website at the time of me writing this, "SageStream, LLC is a credit reporting agency that provides consumer reports and scores regulated by the Fair Credit Reporting Act (FCRA)."

Chex system

This company keeps information on anything to do with bad checks written, An account that has been over-drafted for more than 30 days, or any unpaid overdraft fees. Negative information can report with this credit bureau for up to 5 years.

"Utilize every resource available to you."

CHAPTER 5

Before you send your first dispute...

IF YOU ARE committed to fixing your credit, you have to use every law, and loophole there is to your advantage. Freeze your 3rd party credit bureaus! When you close those doors, you force the credit bureaus to do the leg work and verify your negative accounts. There is no reason to unfreeze these 3rd party credit bureaus after you boost your score, but if you are worried about having them frozen, you can always un-freeze after you increase your score. You Can Freeze your reports by following the instructions below.

Lexis Nexus

https://optout.lexisnexus.com/oo.jsp

Once you opt-out and freeze your report, you want to wait 30 days to ensure the freeze has been placed on your report. Sometimes, the bureaus will have the report frozen sooner than 30 days, but we want to play it 100% safe in this case.

Sage Stream

To freeze sage stream, you must send a letter to them. You can use this exact letter template to send to Sage stream

Adam Smith
1234 ABC Street
Las Vegas Nevada
Birthday: 02/07/1996
SSN: 000-00-0000
Sage Stream LLC

I wish to freeze my credit report with your company. Please Acknowledge my request with a prompt response. Thank you,
Signature

Disputing

During the early stages of the dispute process, it seems as if it is taking forever to get the ball rolling, but I cannot stress how crucial this preparation period is. Do it right the first time, so you do not have to worry about going back and wishing you had done it right the first time.

At this point, you may be wondering, 'what are the best ways to get your credit reports so you can begin disputing?" You can request a free annual credit report from each credit bureau; after that, you must use a reliable credit monitoring service. Free services such as Credit Karma do not offer you enough information about your credit report to implement the strategies in this book. If you want to get access to the best credit monitoring, then go to thecreditreset.com/resources, and you will see a few options to pick from.

Snail Mail or electronic?

Electronic disputing at face value seems as if it was created to benefit the consumer and make disputing an account more simple, but in reality, it was designed to make it easier on the credit bureaus. Just because a few people have gotten accounts removed by doing a quick and easy online dispute does not mean you should go this route. Understand that this is the exception to the rule, and we want to give ourselves that highest chance of success. Snail mail has withstood the test of time, and it is the form of disputing that yields the best results. Also, when disputing an account online, you forfeit your right to receive the results of the credit bureau investigation in writing.

Disputing through the phone can be useful when you are getting old addresses removed. Still, other than that, snail mail leaves a paper trail, and it puts the most pressure on the credit bureaus to respond in the time frame that the FCRA requires them to do so.

Get rid of anything attaching you to negative accounts...

Clean up your credit reports, delete any inaccurate or noncurrent names or addresses. When we put pressure on the credit bureaus, original creditors, or collections agencies to verify the negative account in question, it can be as easy looking up your name and address in their database and matching it up to what is on your credit report.

When there are old addresses or inaccurate names on your credit report, it is usually due to either inconsistency, meaning you may be using different names or have moved and not updated all of your addresses information. Your report can have several names and addresses that you have every right to remove and update. A credit report may have five different names on file such as

Bill Jhonson Smith
Bill Smith
Bill Smith IV
Jhonson Smith
Jhonson Smith IV

Once you freeze your 3rd party credit bureaus and update all your information on your credit report, you are going to want to wait 30 days before you send your first dispute to make sure all of the freezes have been placed on the reports. This can make the process seem sluggish, but laying your foundation is incredibly important. Ruining your credit can occur in a single event, maxing out a card, missing one payment, or filing for bankruptcy, but repairing it is a process.

Before you dispute checklist

- **Freeze Your Lexis Nexus Report**
- **Opt-out of Lexis Nexus**
- **Freeze Your Innovis Report**
- **Freeze Your Sage Stream Report**
- **Wait for 30 days to Verify the Freezes**
- **Opt-out of PreScreen Offers**
- **Remove any incorrect names**
- **Remove all old addresses**

CHAPTER **6**

Collection agencies

COLLECTION AGENCIES ARE 3rd party agencies that the original creditor brings into the picture when a debtor does not pay as agreed.

Usually, collection agencies buy debt in bulk, and with that comes the accounting records of the accounts they are attempting to collect payment on. I am sure you have heard "credit gurus" give the same, "Never pay a collections account" advice. The gurus never tell you why and it doesn't make sense because the debt is yours, but I am not going to sit here and tell you never to pay a collections account because there is a time and place that paying a collection account makes a lot of sense. For instance, if you have been unsuccessful in disputing the account off of your credit report. If you can negotiate a 'pay for deletion letter,' this is an agreement between you and the collection agency that states they will delete the negative entry off of your credit report. The deletion will happen once you pay down the entire balance. If you ever go this route, make sure you get everything in writing, and you want to communicate through the mail. Make sure you are very careful with your language to make sure you are not admitting that you owe the debt.

If that situation is not your case, there is no need ever to pay a collections agency without two things, proof that you originated the debt and chain of title. Ask yourself, can the collections agency prove it is you who created the debt? They might respond to a dispute you send with a screenshot of some accounting records, but that simply is not enough to prove you are the one responsible for the debt. As stated earlier, the collections agencies often buy debt in bulk, and they purchase the accounting records to go with it. Still, they often do not have the chain of title. The chain of title is what legally allows debt collectors to collect on a debt

It is just a complicated way of saying who has been assigned the debt in the past and who is currently assigned to the debt (A sold to B sold to C sold to D). It MUST be proven that the person calling you is the person or company that is legally able to collect on this debt. You never hear people who are victims of collections agencies say anything like, "I was getting harassing debt collector calls, and I asked them for the proof of the chain of title in writing, and they stopped calling me." You don't hear that because collection agencies thrive off of the ignorance of consumers.

Collections agencies will tell you anything over the phone and sound as if they are on your side, but they are not on your side in reality. Collection agencies want to collect payment from you at all costs. So, they will lie, ask you about your personal life to build a relationship with you, scare you with complex language and legal terms. These people do not care about your financial mistakes, hardships, or anything else, so stop donating your money to these agencies without exercising your rights. Usually, the collection agents on the phone work based on commission, and they are given a lot of leeways when it comes to what tactics they can use to collect money.

A family friend of mine saved up $20,000 to pay a collections account. They hoped that their score would rise after they paid. After spending hours at work, making money that could have gone toward their family's betterment that the entire $20,000 was DONATED to the collections agency. This person didn't look to do debt settlement or negotiate a pay for deletion letter just $20,000 gone bye-bye. Use this script when debt collectors call you so you can avoid this...

> **"Thank you for calling me about this.**
> **I had no idea about it.**
> **Can I have the reference number for this account, your company name, and your mailing address?**
> **I do not want to receive any phone calls about this issue any longer.**
> **I would like to receive all future correspondence via mail.**
> **Can you send me something in the mail to the address you have on file? Preferably the chain of title and any proof regarding this.**
> **If they persist with questions or make any claims, keep repeating the script and stay calm! You cannot budge on this, and you cannot begin answering questions."**
> **Remember, If it's not in writing, it's not real!**

Side note…

If your mortgage consultant tells you to be approved for your home loan, you need to pay a collections account; pay it. Your loan officer is the person who can secure your loan, and if he or she is telling you explicitly that the account in question needs to be paid to secure your loan, pay it. In that case, it is not donating; you need to do that to secure your home loan or some other kind of bank loan.

Debt settlement

If you are in a situation where a collections account must be paid, then debt settlement will allow you to get the collections agency off of your back at a discounted rate. Debt settlement is when you offer to pay less than you owe on a debt. Most collections agencies will take 40 cents on the dollar; that would give you a 40% discount. Keep in mind when you settle on a debt, the IRS will look at the amount that was unpaid as earned taxable income, and you will be receiving a 1099-C form in the mail. I do not recommend people go this route because it will lower your chances of getting a pay for deletion letter. Settling your debt will not increase your score. If you do end up settling on debt, do not pay with anything tied to your banking accounts. Some collections agencies will extract that entire balance owed out of your bank account. Like I said, all collections agencies care about it collecting payment at all costs. Regardless, It is essential to know your options when dealing with collection agencies.

Collection Agency Checklist

- Only communicate with a collection agency by mail
- Never admit that you owe a debt
- Always demand proof that they can collect on a debt
- Never give them any extra information (Banking, Signature)
- If You Settle On A debt pay with a money order or a prepaid visa debit card

CHAPTER 7

Where do I start?

WHEN IT COMES to disputing your negative accounts, keep in mind under FCRA law you, as the consumer, have the right to dispute anything inaccurate, erroneous, or unverifiable. The Credit bureaus expect you not to understand anything about the credit repair process and not even understand half of everything in the dispute letters. Go over Section 604, 605B, 609, 611, and 623, and the Fair debt collection practices act. If you have problems finding these, you can go to www.thecreditreset/resources, and you will be able to access those

After understanding the basics of the law, there is a specific order you are going to want to dispute your negative items in, and that is...

1. Debts Past The Statute Of Limitations

During the credit repair process, you have to make sure you use every law to your advantage and make sure you dispute accounts with caution. Before you dispute an account, check the statute of limitations for your debt type and match it up against the last date of the activity. You may find that some accounts are not worth disputing. In addition to this, when it comes to the statute of limitations and what is considered activity on an account can be tricky and disputing, it can be considered activity. You can go to www.thecreditreset/resources and download a free copy of the statute of limitations.

2. Paid Accounts

You will find that paid accounts are easier because that specific creditor has gotten what they want, and that is their money. Start with everything that is a paid account. Example: Paid Public Record, Paid Tax Lien, Paid Medical accounts Paid off closed accounts. This section does not include paid off collection accounts.

3. Unpaid Accounts

After all your paid accounts, you can start to attack those unpaid accounts. Keep in mind just because an account has been removed from your credit report, it doesn't mean that money is no longer owed. Contracts to pay debts and credit reporting are two different things.

4. Collections accounts

You will have to play hardball with the collections agencies, which will likely be your most challenging battles. You can use many different strategies when dealing with collection agencies, and we'll go into detail on this later.

5. Late Payments and Inquiries

Late Payments are not impossible to get removed, but it

often requires the whole account to be removed from your credit report. Depending on how often you were late on that account and how long it has been open will determine your next move. If you have an account that has been open for six years and it has one late payment, it isn't worth losing six years of credit history over one late payment. You really shouldn't worry about inquiries; they don't affect your score after 24 months. If you need to get the inquiries removed to qualify for a home or some funding reason, you can go ahead and get those removed.

1st Round

Your first dispute should always be short and straightforward. In the first round, we want to get the credit bureaus to respond. When you send this letter, you might even see some accounts be removed from your credit report during this stage of the dispute process because the accounts we are disputing first are paid accounts. As mentioned earlier, when creditors have their money, you are usually met with less resistance. Here is what a 1st Round letter looks like...

Vernell Watts
123 ABC Street
000-00-0000
Bureau_address
Current Date
To Whom It May Concern,

This letter is a formal complaint that you are reporting inaccurate and incomplete credit information on my Credit Report.

I understand that mistakes happen but your inaccurate information could cost me in higher interest rates and I have enough expenses as it is. Please investigate the following information and either remove it or at least send me the information that you used to add it to my report.

(Dispute Explanation)
Sincerely yours,
SIGNATURE

Watch out for E Oscar...

E oscar is a software that the credit bureaus added to their system in 1993. The reason the credit bureaus who own this software, Equifax, Experian, Transunion, and Innovis, added it was to cut cost and automate the majority of the dispute process. According to the E-Oscar Website, this is what the software does;" e-OSCAR is a web-based, Metro2 compliant, automated system that enables Data Furnishers (DFs), and Credit Reporting Agencies (CRAs) to create and respond to consumer credit history disputes. CRAs include Equifax, Experian, Innovis, and TransUnion, their affiliates, or Independent Credit Bureaus and Mortgage Reporting Companies. e-OSCAR also provides for DFs to send "out-of-cycle" credit history updates to CRAs." The website also mentions, "The system primarily supports Automated Credit Dispute Verification (ACDV) and Automated Universal Dataform (AUD) processing as well as a number of related processes that handle registration, subscriber code management, and reporting."

In short, The E oscar software processes each dispute and attaches a code to it and puts it in a category and automates the "verification." Here are the most important ones...

1. **Not mine (001)**
2. **Inaccurate information (112)**
3. **Balances (109)**
4. **Account Closed (024)**

Scare Tactics

There is a chance that after you send, you will receive a response much like…

"We received a suspicious request regarding your credit file. We have determined that this request was not made by you and we have not taken any action
Requests made in this manner in the future will not be processed and will not receive a response."

This response never makes any sense because you should be attaching a copy of a recent bill and a copy of your driver's license. The bureaus may also send you something along the lines of...

"Suspicious requests are taken seriously and reviewed by security personnel who will report dece[tive activity, including letters deemed as suspicious to law enforcement officials and to state or federal regulatory agencies."

The responses shown above are nothing but scare and stall tactics that the credit bureaus use to make you give up. Keep applying pressure to the credit bureaus to get a response.

Can I sue?

If the credit bureaus refuse to respond to you, you can file a lawsuit. File your complaint at https://ftccomplaintassistant.gov

Bringing in the CFPB can also help you in this situation. It is known to be less effective than filing a complaint with the FTC, but bringing in the CFPB can only help you in this situation. You can contact them at https://www.consumerfinance.gov/complaint/

Quick tip...

After you send your first round of dispute letters, you want to be very specific in what you want the credit bureaus to do in the next round of letters. Make sure to mention whether you want an account updated or removed. If you do not tell the credit bureaus what to do, they will do nothing.

2nd Round

After we nudge the credit bureaus to get a response, we can see exactly what we're working with. Some accounts may have fallen off after your first round it, but often the credit bureaus will send an automatic response that the account was verified, and it remains. Fear not because it is likely that they did not do an actual investigation on your behalf. This is when we start to put pressure on the credit bureaus and ask them for a method of verification on the account. This is a way to see what they investigated, and at this point, this is where the creditors will usually try to use the name and addresses tied to the account that correlates with the credit report. Here is what a push letter looks like…

Vernell Watts
1234 ABC Street
000-00-0000
(Bureau Address)
(Current Date)
To Whom It May Concern:

I am concerned about the validity and accuracy of your recent investigation of these accounts that are reporting on my credit report. 30 days ago I requested an investigation because I felt the item(s) below were not being reported legally. A Couple of days ago I received a letter stating that your investigation was complete. Please explain to me how you conducted your investigation!

Please explain to me what your representatives uncovered to lead them to believe that you are reporting this item as it legally should be reported?

What certified documents were reviewed to

conclude your investigation?

Please provide a complete copy of all of the information that was transmitted to the data furnisher as part of the investigation.

What did it cost your company to obtain the documents needed to complete your investigation?

Please provide proof of your timely procurement of certified documents.

Did you speak directly to any employee of the company that was reporting the information to confirm the accuracy of what you are reporting?

If yes to above:

Who did you speak to?

On what date?

How long was the conversation?

What was their position?

What telephone number did you call?

What is the name of the employee of your company that spoke directly to the above party?

What is the position of the employee of your company that spoke directly to the above party?

How long has that employee been employed at your company?

What formal training was provided to this employee to investigate items of this kind?

Was there any e-mail or written communication between members of your company and the above party?

If so, please provide copies of all correspondence; supply copies of any and all conclusive documentation to prove that

you have in fact conducted a reasonable investigation of the account in question.

Provide the date of the commencement of delinquency

Provide the specific date reporting that these items will cease

Enclosed with your response to the above questions I respectfully request a notarized affidavit confirming the information that is provided is accurate as per my civil rights granted under several federal laws. This information should not come as a form letter response.

My initial dispute was detailed and directly related to the account in question. A template response will not be an acceptable response. If you cannot supply ALL of the above information in a timely manner as detailed in several laws, including but not limited to the Fair Credit Reporting Act, I must immediately demand the permanent removal of this item from my credit report.

This erroneous entry is hurting my overall credit rating and has caused me severe financial and emotional distress. If you choose not to provide the above-requested deletion or requested/required documentation of your investigation, I will pursue the enforcement of my constitutional rights via federal court proceedings. As you are well aware this information will come out through my formal discovery process and necessary depositions. I have recently studied

constitutional consumer protection laws along with civil/federal court procedures.
Please respond accordingly,

Signature

3rd round

If the account has made it to the 3rd round, it is time to pull out the big guns and get specific. This round, we will put pressure on the credit bureaus to have several aspects of an account investigated instead of the account and its entirety. In the last round, we questioned their investigation; next, we need to examine different parts of the account. This is used to overwhelm the credit bureaus. Here is what a letter for this round looks

Vernell Watts
123 ABC Street
Transunion
P.O. Box 2000
Chester, PA 19016-2000
RE: American Express Credit Card

To whom it may concern,
 I have Obtained my credit report and I have noticed several errors on the account
 I have never been 90 days late please remove this
 This is being reported as an open account, please remove this
 No payment was made in 5/2010

The date of the first delinquency with original creditors is not provided please provide this

The card limit is reporting as $3,000 which is incorrect please correct this

Please correct or remove this information as this incorrect information is damaging my financial situation and causing great financial distress. Please respond within the legal timeframe stated in the FCRA. A template response will not be an acceptable response. I await your response.

Signature

CHAPTER 8

If it didn't work

IF THE 3 round nudge, push, shove did not work, this does not mean it is game over. I would be surprised if you told me it didn't, but it does happen. Other angels take a bit more time and patience. Mark your calendar for 60 days and stop disputing during that time. With each of the credit bureaus having more than one address sometimes they shut down their addresses to slow up the dispute process

After those 60 days are up, it is time to tackle those stubborn accounts differently. You can dispute different aspects of the tradeline using separate letters and dispute them on separate days. Other elements of an account that can be are Account Number Date Opened Credit Limit High credit limit Term Length Status Balance Past due balance Date of last payment Date of last activity Date closed Charge-off amount Type of account (installment, revolving, open) Ownership (joint account, individual, authorized user). This chart will show you exactly how this process works.

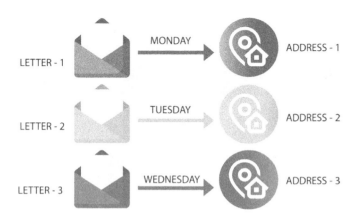

Late Payments

Dealing with late payments can be tricky. Getting the entire account removed from your credit report, but this could also lower your score. You have two options when it comes to late payments...

- **Have The Entire Account Removed**

This will get rid of all of the payment history; both positive and negative

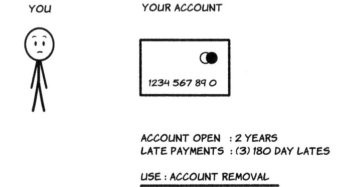

- **Ask For An Account Update**

This is one of the hardest things to accomplish. Doing this would remove the negative payment history, and the positive will remain. Here is how you know which strategy to use...

YOU   **YOUR ACCOUNT**

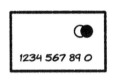

ACCOUNT OPEN   : 10 YEARS
LATE PAYMENTS : (2) 30 DAY LATES

USE : ACCOUNT UPDATE

Dealing With Bankruptcy

Many credit repair professionals and people looking to repair their credit on their own will not even deal with bankruptcy. Most people are scared of anything that comes from a courthouse, but the bankruptcy has already taken place; it won't ruin your credit if you dispute it.

Now depending on whether you filed a chapter 7 bankruptcy, which would wipe all of your debt and will report for up to 10 years, or you filed a chapter 13 bankruptcy, which would put you on a wage earners repayment plan, and that would report for seven years. Now, if you have been considering filing for bankruptcy, seek an attorney. I am not an attorney, and this is not legal advice

Sending a letter challenging the bankruptcy and its entirety claiming it is not yours or didn't file for bankruptcy never works. What yields better results is challenging the specifics of the bankruptcy to have it removed. You can challenge the date filed, or what type of bankruptcy was filed. You can use the same 1,2,3 round strategy for bankruptcy. Swap out the words and change up the phrasing as it pertains to your situation.

Reinsertions

When you are successful in getting your accounts removed, there is a chance 1 or 2 might pop back up on your credit report. There is no specific reason that this happens since it violates section 611 of the FCRA. Section 611 states *'the information may not be reinserted in the file by the consumer reporting agency unless the person who furnishes the information certifies that the information is complete and accurate." Section 611 also states, "Consumer reporting agency shall notify the consumer of the reinsertion in writing not later than five business days after insertion."*

If you did not receive a notice of reinsertion, then your FCRA rights have been violated, and you can request removal. When seeing reinsertions, it can make you feel as if all your hard work has gone to waste. Though it may feel like it was a waste, this is not the case; We know the credit bureaus are not putting their best foot forward to make sure accounts are reporting accurately. The likelihood of you receiving notice of reinsertion in the five business day timeframe is slim to none. You can find the letters to have reinsertions removed in the dispute letter section.

Dealing with Medical collections

Medical emergencies happen, and often when you least expect. Medical emergencies are why so many people have had the displeasure of having their medical bill sent to collections. Luckily, Medical collections are often some of the easiest accounts to remove. The HIPPA laws make sure to keep your information safe from the collections agency. HIPAA laws, which stands for Health Insurance Portability and Accountability Act, makes it hard for the collections agency to verify the account. With the account being hard to verify, the result is a removal. Though this is true, I am in no way saying you should rack up medical bills and never pay the bill.

The same dispute strategies can be applied to this, and letters specific to medical accounts can be found in the dispute letter section.

Dealing with inquiries

For the most part, inquiries do not significantly impact your score if you get them within reason. I have heard of car dealerships running their clients credit 30-40 times to get them a loan. If this happens to you, you won't be able to get any other line of credit. This includes home loans, credit cards, retail credit lines, nothing. There is a way you can have all these inquires removed, though. Here are some things to consider before using these strategies...

1. If The inquiry is tied to an open account and you get the inquiry removed it will close the account
2. If the inquiry was more than 12 months ago, you

would be wasting your time because, after 12 months, the inquiry has minimal effect on your credit score. After 24 months, the inquiry won't affect your score at all.

According to the FCRA, no persons may obtain a consumer credit report unless it is for a "permissible purpose." Here is what is considered 'permissible purpose."

1. Consumers written consent
2. The consumer is extended some form of credit
3. Making a hiring decision
4. Underwriting for insurance
5. To find out whether or not you still qualify for an open account

For a creditor to have proof of permissible purpose, they must have proof that you initiated the inquiry and written authorization. Creditors only have this after you have an account open with them. Here is the type of letter you would use to dispute inquiries...

The Unfair Advantage

If one of your issues is credit card debt, I've been there. The whole world is buying now and paying later, so it is easy to fall into that trap, then struggle daily. Before I get into any strategies to help you with this, there are two concepts you must understand. The first one is, you must change your habits; none of what I will say will work if you do not change your habits. Number two; most of this only works after you have improved your credit. This is why I have this section after the disputing section. Now that's out the way; let's get into some way you can pay your debt off faster.

Find out what your interest rate is. Most people have no idea how long it will take for the card to be paid off at the rate they are paying or; how much interest they are paying. Most are scared and or embarrassed to look at that statement and feel like they will never climb their way out of debt. This is entirely understandable, especially when one month you owed $2,000, and the next month you owed $2,200. You have been through much worse than numbers on a piece of paper face the problem so you can execute the solution.

Negotiate your interest rates and any fees. Nearly everything is negotiable when it comes to your credit card, and if you are wondering, "how the heck could I negotiate?" Simple contact the support line for your card provider and say, "I got a preapproval in the mail that offered a __% interest on a balance transfer. Now I would prefer to keep my balance with you guys and avoid opening a new card, but I was wondering what can you do for me in this situation?" The more leverage you have in a situation like this, the better. Mention things like your payment history with the company (if it's good), how long you've had an account with them, or anything that might convince the person on the phone to get you a lower rate. Negotiating fees such as annual fees will depend on your relationship with the bank. When I could not afford the $500 annual fee on my Platinum card, I called the support line to see if they could help. When I called, I said: "I've been using American Express products since the day I turned 18, and I am not in the position to pay the annual fee. Now I want to keep this card, and I was wondering what you guys can do to help me?" Do not say, "is there anything you can do to help me out?" Keep the question open-ended so that you keep your options open; maybe they waive the fee; perhaps they cut it in half or push it to the next billing month.

Use balance transfers to your advantage. Now depending on your age of credit, opening a new account could drop your score significantly. I would take the dip in my score rather than being caught up in the hamster wheel of paying the minimum payment while the balance continues to increase. You may be asking, "what happens if I get denied?" you're still in the game, don't worry. Find the reconsideration line number for the card company you applied to and ask them why wasn't your application approved and what they can do to get it approved. While you are talking to the rep, keep in mind how many people are calling them daily who are pissed off because they were denied. Remain polite, and you could even go as far as trying to make a friend. We will dive into this topic later on.

Respect your money Even if you have a lower income, it's likely you're consuming way beyond your means or else you wouldn't be in this situation. I get it, and I have been there; you may be out at a mall or out and about town or maybe even see something new gadget you like on Amazon. You don't have the money for it now, but there is a credit card with a $2,000 limit on it in your pocket. The more you get into the habit of doing this, it will create a snowball effect of debt. Have a tight budget and try not even carry credit cards with you while you're out if you don't plan on paying it off in full at the end of the month

Look into personal loans. Depending on your financial situation, this could be a great option. Now using debt to pay debt seems like a bad idea until you consider that high credit card balances are negatively affecting your score. Fixed payment loans, aka installment loans, do not count against your utilization.

Student Loans

Depending on what kind of student loans you have, there is a good chance the loans cannot be discharged in bankruptcy. Only certain loan types and hardship qualifications will allow you to discharge your student loans in bankruptcy. Seek out a bankruptcy attorney to get more information on this. Someone is going to have to pay back these loans. These loans often have a high-interest rate because most people who have student loans got them at a young age where they may have had no credit activity. There are different forgiveness programs and programs that allow those who have fallen behind on their student loan payments. At the time of writing this, there are 44 million Americans who have 1.3 Trillion in student debt, with the average debt being $37,000.

I believe in education, and there is a need for professionals in our communities such as Doctors, Lawyers, Engineers, and any other professional practice that requires college. Still, it is sad to see college graduates that have degrees in communications, Music history, or something else ridiculous working at whole foods with $30,000 in debt. They could have gotten that job right out of high school. It never makes sense to give an 18 a year old that knows nothing about how credit and interest works tens of thousands of dollars in unsecured loans for a degree that they are not even 100% sure on. The example above is the reality of student loans, unfortunately. There are options to help with student loans as long as they haven't already been sent to collections.

Deferment: When your loan is in deferment, it puts a temporary pause on the payments. Usually, interest is still accumulating when the loan is in deferment; some loans do not accumulate interest. Still, you will want to check with your loan servicer. Deferment could buy you some time to get together a strategy to tackle your student loans.

Forbearance: Federal or private student loans can be put into forbearance if you cannot service the loan due to a hardship. The loan will still accumulate interest during the forbearance period. During forbearance, you can comb through all of your expenses and figure out how to make extra money to help you service the loan.

Rehabilitation: Usually, a nine-month repayment program where you must pay as agreed. Rehabilitation will help your loan get out of default status. After nine months of paying as agreed, the loan servicer will remove the negative entries on your credit report concerning that loan.

There are other industry-specific programs, such as teacher forgiveness. These programs change and are very industry-specific. Seek out an attorney who specializes in student loans to get more information about forgiveness programs.

Just like any other debt, if you ignore the issue, it will only get worse. Understand where you're at with your student loans. After you figure out where you are, you must figure out where you need to be to get through this.

CHAPTER 9

The Homeownership Blueprint

IF YOUR GOAL is to own a home, the 3 C blueprint will be the framework to achieve homeownership in any market. As you begin to prepare for homeownership, you must always come back to the 3 Cs. The 3 C blueprint is what ALL lenders are looking for regardless of which state you live in. The 3 C's are...

- **Credit**

Having a strong credit score is very important when buying a home for obvious reasons, but, more importantly, you have to build a strong credit file. I will break down exactly how to do this in the next section.

CREDIT SCORE : 760

- **Capacity**

No matter how high your credit score is, you have to service the loan; we call this capacity. It wouldn't make sense to go through all this trouble to get a house just so the house can eat up all of your money. You don't want to overextend yourself.

I CAN AFFORD
THE PAYMENTS

- **Collateral**

Collateral has less to do with your finances and more to do with the home you choose. The collateral is the home; if a borrower is unable to pay back the loan, the bank will seize the house. When you are getting your loan, the property must be given an appraised value.

This means a 3rd party appraisal professional will help determine the home's value based on; the current market and the home's features (amenities, floor plan, square footage) to determine the property's value.

Even though credit requirements change frequently and can vary from lender to lender, having a strong credit score of 700+ will ALWAYS be a plus in a

THE HOUSE IS WORTH
WHAT I AM
PAYING

lender's eyes. You will either go to two routes when securing your mortgage; you will go through a bank such as a local credit union or use a mortgage broker. One thing to consider when deciding which route to go is, mortgage brokers have a lot more flexibility because they are not tied to one financial institution as opposed to your local credit union. Mortgage brokers can usually work with you closely to help you meet the underwriting requirements. Get In contact with our team through email at support@fortune800.com to help connect you with the best realtor/mortgage broker in your area.

CHAPTER 10

Rebuilding Your Credit Report

No score? No problem

IF YOU HAD a lot negatively reporting accounts and little to no positively reporting accounts at the start of your credit repair journey, you have gone into a credit reset mode. You're in a great position here because you are only one or two approvals away from a 700+ credit score.

Often, when people repair their credit or pay a company to do it, they are left with a "thin credit file." If you want to own a home having a thin credit profile will not work; you will be denied. You must demonstrate that you have or can be responsible with your credit. Here are the stages of building your credit...

Step One

Know your options: Having no credit is just like having

bad credit, so getting your first cards after repairing your credit can be challenging; here are your three choices when establishing initial credit.

Merchant Card

This is a credit card that can only be used with a specific merchant. This can be an online retailer or in a physical location. When you hear a merchant card think Macy's card, Gap Card, or Fingerhut card, these are a good option because these creditors give higher credit limits, and the lines of credit are unsecured. When a credit line is unsecured, that means you do not have to put any upfront money to get the credit card. Though this is true, the retailer will usually have you buy something to get the line of credit. These are a great option to establish an unsecured *primary account*. Keep reading, and you find out why having *primary accounts* is a must.

Secured Credit Card

A secured card is a credit line that is secured by your collateral, aka your money. If you make a $300 deposit with a credit card company, they will extend you a $300 credit line. Once you have shown that you can be responsible with the credit card, the company will return your deposit. Secured cards are also a great option to get a primary account reporting on your credit file.

Before I explain the last option, I want to break down the difference between a primary user and an authorized user account. Because I am sure you are wondering, "What does he mean by primary account?"

A Primary Account is a credit card account that is 100%

in your name. You applied for the card in your name, with your SSN. These accounts have the largest impact on your credit score, and you want to have as many as possible.

An Authorized User Account is an account that someone else owns. Let say one of your friends or family members has a credit card with a $10,000 limit. They have been making on-time payments for ten years and only use $100 per month on the card. Your friend or family member can add you on to the card as an authorized user, and now that $10,000 card will report on your credit file, in turn boosting your score. Sounds great, doesn't it? Well, there's a catch… Kind of…

When I first turned 18, I got my first credit cards through being an authorized user. I had a solid score of 717, and I was excited. I was excited that I called CarMax and decided to see if I could qualify for a BMW. In my head, I am thinking, "I qualify since my score is high," I could not have been more wrong. The sales rep on the phone said, "no banks are willing to give you a loan" I said, "Why I have a 717 credit score" he replied, "I am not sure maybe because you are young." Neither one of us knew why I didn't qualify, but looking back on it, I realized; it was because my entire credit report was made of authorized users. None of the accounts were actually mine. So I had a useless 700+ credit score.

Authorized users

If you have a friend, family member, or a trusted company that can help you get some authorized user accounts reporting, do it! It does help but understand; the goal is always to get primary accounts.

What Is Blending

Blending is a concept I came up with when I began to build a healthy credit file. It isn't a crazy complicated concept; all it requires is simple math and proper planning. If you want a 700+ score, this is the fastest way to do it; it is the exact formula we use for our clients. For every authorized user account you get, you have two primary accounts. You can blend easily using the merchant and secured card strategy. When you blend the authorized user accounts and the primary accounts, you can quickly build an excellent looking credit file.

Here is an example of how blending can work

Joe just got his credit repaired; he was able to get negative accounts removed, but he didn't have any positive accounts. So in the eyes of the creditors, he still has terrible credit.

Joe goes and gets a merchant card from an online retail shop. The retailer extends him a $1,500 line of credit. Since the card can only be used with that retailer, Joe only uses the card once. After this, he goes and gets a secured card with a $300 line of credit, and he only spends 20 bucks a month on it.

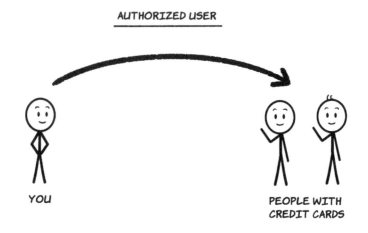

AUTHORIZED USER

YOU

PEOPLE WITH
CREDIT CARDS

After this, Joe Seeks out an authorized user account; he asks his responsible friends and family members and also seeks out a professional company that can help him with this. He is able to get added to a $10,000 card. Joe has now built a solid credit file and moves on to step 2...

Step Two

Step two only requires one thing, and that is discipline. Like I mentioned earlier, a lot of credit "gurus" will tell you that you need to keep your utilization right under 30%, but now that you have read this book, you know that this won't help your credit score. You must keep your utilization between 1-7% if you want this process to move quickly.

Getting Cards from the big banks

When you get your first lines of credit from big banks such as American Express, Citi Bank, Capital One, Discover, etc, they will issue you small credit lines. These Credit Lines will range from $500-$1,000; as I mentioned earlier, you want to make sure you are only using 1-7% of the total available credit line.

Step Three

Ask For Credit Line Increases and continue to apply step two. I have seen the most success with asking for $3,000 at a time. This means if I have a $1,000 credit limit, I will ask the creditor to increase it to $4,000. Do not open any new credit at this stage. Just focus on increasing the lines of credit you have. I have seen people go and get ten credit cards with a $1,000 limit to make it seem like they have a lot of credit;

in reality, if that person were to apply for a home loan, they would look like a compulsive or desperate borrower. No new lines of credit until you have got all of your starter credit cards to at least $6,000 each.

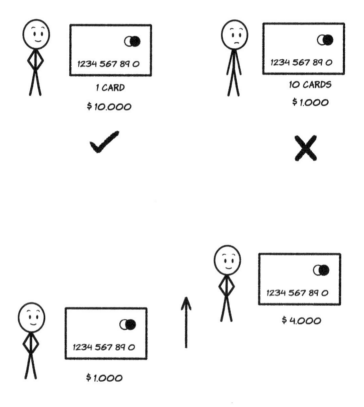

Step Four

Step four is optional; if you would like to upgrade your cards for cashback benefits, flight benefits, or any other kind of benefits, you can ask the credit card company for product upgrades. Each starter credit card has an upgrade; here's an example...

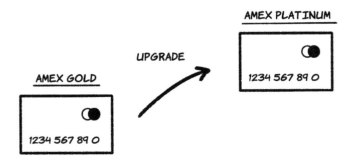

CHAPTER 11

Homebuyer Check List

ONE MISTAKE A lot of potential home buyers make is they enter the process blindly. They have not thoroughly gone through their finances; they haven't checked their credit score. A lot of people contact a lender, apply for a loan, and pray. A home is likely the largest purchase you and I will make in our life; with that said, it doesn't make sense not to have a strategy. Here are things you must do before you contact a realtor or a loan officer...

1. **Check Your FICO Score, Not Credit Karma**

As I mentioned earlier, there is a difference between your FICO score and your FAKO score. Lenders do not use your Credit Karma score; they use your FICO score. You can request a free annual report from each credit bureau.

2. **Lower Your Debt To Income Ratio**

Debt to income ratio is important because it correlates with the Capacity portion of the 3 C blueprint mentioned earlier. If you are overextended on credit cards, car loans, or any other credit lines, you will be denied.

3. Get To 1%-7% In Credit Card Usage

I know I know I've mentioned this a lot at this point, but this is important. It will improve your credit score and keep you Debt To Income Ratio Low.

What You Shouldn't Do

Now that we have discussed what you should do, we need to also discuss what you shouldn't do…

1. Close Old Accounts

When it comes to credit card debt, a lot of people are frustrated, understandably. Some people will work hard, pay off an account, and close the account. Doing this will lower your credit score; here is an example…

Let's say you have two credit cards that each have a $2,000 limit, so you have $4,000 in credit line. At the same time, both cards are maxed out; you have a 100% usage rate. Then, you pay one card off completely now; your usage rate is 50%. You decide to close the account you paid off now instead of having a $4,000 credit limit; you have a $2,000 credit; now, your usage is back to 100%.

By now, I am sure you can understand why keeping your accounts open is important.

2. Pay Off Instalment Loans

Doing this will help your debt to income ratio, but it will temporarily lower your credit score, but there is an alternative.

You can call the finance company that extended you the loan and pay the loan down to one dollar. After this, you can ask them if you can schedule the last payment on the last payment date. This way, you have lowered your debt to income ratio but not your credit score.

3. Add To Your Credit Card Debt

If you are committed to changing your financial future, committed to achieving homeownership, and you must change your financial habits. If you usually charge up your credit cards without a second thought, that ends today… Of course, only if you are committed instead of interested. Then again, this isn't a budgeting or financial discipline book, but I got you covered; go to www.thecreditreset/resources to get access to a free budgeting template.

Building Your Real Estate Team

If you have applied 100% of what I said in the previous chapter, you are now ready to start building your real estate team. As you are going through the home buying process, you have to look at it like building a sports team. Each player has a different role and to achieve homeownership. Your team will Consist of…

The Realtor

The Mortgage Broker

Title Company/ Lawyer

Property Inspector

The Realtor will act as the point guard or the quarterback for your team. Some potential homebuyers will not work with a realtor for whatever reason, but there are no benefits in not working with a realtor. Realtors have access to what's on the market in real-time, instead of a service like Zillow that may show you homes that have already been sold. In addition to this, the realtor will help you find the house in your price range and negotiate with the seller's agent.

On the other hand, not all agents are created equal. Some agents do not know much about the process and don't communicate with clients effectively. If you already know a rockstar agent awesome, building the rest of your team will be easy. If you don't know a rockstar agent, we know plenty! Contact us at info@fortune800.com, and we can connect you with the best agent in your area.

The Mortgage Broker will score the touchdown or dunk the ball because you cannot get a home without the money. Usually, rockstar agents only work with rockstar lenders, so the agent will connect you with the best lender.

The Title Company/lawyer will review the title, help with any insurance policies, and handle the closing paperwork.

The property inspector can end up being the unsung hero. Making sure the physical condition of the home is suitable. This prevents surprise last-minute costs that may prevent you from being able to close on your home.

CHAPTER 12

Putting It All Together

AT THIS POINT, you are likely feeling one of two ways; you're super excited to implement all of the strategies in this book, or you are feeling overwhelmed by the information. If you are overwhelmed, understand this book is not a one time read. This book can act as a guide for you. This is going to take time, but the results are worth the wait.

How To Get More Help

If you are thinking, "I don't want to do all this, I just want a professional to help me," we got you covered. We implement these strategies for our clients and handle all of this. We handle the disputes, we have authorized user cards our clients can access, merchant cards, and secured cards. Go to www.fortune800.com to get a free credit analysis. Me or one of our team members can hop on a call with you and see if you are a good fit for our program.

CHAPTER 13

Playing The Credit Game

FOR THOSE WHO want to do more than buy a home with their credit I wanted to add this bonus section to the book. Once you have applied all the information in the book, congratulations, you are in the 700s club. You will enjoy low-interest rates, instant approvals, and negotiation power. Life with a 700+ score gives you peace of mind as you won't have to take shortcuts when you have to use your name. There will be no more cosigners, no more ridiculous deposit amounts. There will be no need to feel stressed when you are filling out any kind of credit application.

Buying a Car

Buying a car with a 700+ credit score is simple, and the process is a lot smoother. When you buy a car, it is ALWAYS better to get approved for the amount of car you can afford at a credit union. Once you get that approval, head down to the dealership and shop for the car you preselected after doing an online search. Do not walk into the dealership without an idea of what you are looking for. The car salesmen will usually push buyers who walk into the car dealership without an idea of what they want, how much they want to pay or what kind of interest rate they are looking for toward the cars that are just sitting on the lot that they cannot get rid of for whatever reason.

You must understand all your options on a purchase such as a car, which is a more significant purchase than most people realize. If you get financing through a dealership rather than going to a credit union to get a loan freeze your lowest credit score beforehand. Most dealerships pull from all three bureaus. If the dealership pulls your scores from two bureaus and they are your highest ones, it can help you negotiate lower interest rates. The two bureaus they pulled from will still give them enough accurate information to decide on whether or not you are approved or not.

Don't Rely on this

Getting a car loan will not be enough to help increase your score and improve your credit report. You will still need to get revolving accounts on your credit report. If you stop paying on your car, the company that financed it will repossess it. When you have a card and max it out, and you don't pay, they don't seize anything; the account is charged-off or sent to collections. Collateral is one of the reasons why revolving accounts impact your score more.

Applying for credit

Getting unsecured loans and unsecured lines of credit with a 700+ score will put you in a position of power. You have the power to choose what products best suit your financial needs. Credit cards become a fun game once you know what you are looking for and what benefits you want from each card. When it comes to the credit card game, it can be a dangerous game. It can leave you drowning in debt and thinking you are winning when it is your creditors that are the ones winning. Your goal with credit cards should be to ditch the debt card altogether and only carry your credit cards to maximize your points and rewards. If you do not have the discipline to set a spending limit that will you can pay off in full at the end of every month, do not even worry about this chapter. For those with a bit of discipline, you will be able to enjoy travel rewards, Cashback, and special cardmember offers on purchases you would have made either way.

Do not fall for this trap...

Have you ever been to the grocery store doing routine shopping and maybe you saw the cucumbers were 4 for 3 dollars, now you don't need four cucumbers. You usually don't ever buy any, but since they are on sale, you go ahead and get 4 of them. Fast forward two weeks later, you haven't eaten any of the cucumbers, and they have rottened in your fridge, but hey, at least you got them on sale. This same dynamic takes place when it comes to credit card rewards, "Ooooo look Ammex is giving 20 dollars back for every 50 spent at dominions." That person will spend 50 on dominos pizza that they would not have spent. Still, because of the 20 dollars cash back "deal," it is justified. This trap can drain your bank account quickly. Make sure you are getting points for things you would buy anyway, not stuff you are buying solely because of the reward or promotion.

When it comes to picking the cards that are right for you to consider your lifestyle, if you never leave your city, you do not need a frequent flyer card. If you never dine out, it just wouldn't make sense to have a card that offers you rewards that offer dining rewards. What do you want?

Cash Back

Cards such as the Citi Double Cash offers cash back right into your bank account. Cashback is my personal favorite because it allows me to get cold hard cash for the things I was already going to buy. Most of the cashback hard have 0 or very low annual fees. I pay no annual fees for the cards that offer high cashback percentages.

Travel Rewards

If you want to travel for free or for very little, we will go into detail on exactly how you can do this using credit cards. Travel reward cards are an excellent option for people who dream of traveling the world, seeing new sites, and accumulating more experiences. Travel can come at a high price tag, but if done the right way, you can see the whole world without breaking the bank.

High credit limits

High credit limits allow you to carry balances if you have a legitimate reason to do so. When you have $10,000-$, 20,000 credit card limits your score will not take a massive hit if you have four cards with a combined limit of 60,000, and there is a balance of 3,000 on them. Your score won't be affected because your utilization would only be 5%. If you do not trust yourself with that much credit just focus on one of the other two options

Getting the highest score possible

If getting the best score you can get is your goal, you are going to have to play the long game. That means picking and choosing your credit cards carefully. That means rarely opening new accounts. That means to keep your utilization very low. We will talk about exactly how to get to that 800+ score in a later chapter.

Keep in mind when you are choosing what you want most out of your credit cards, you must choose a primary goal. Whatever is secondary will have to take a back seat because going for one category of rewards will make it nearly impossible to go for another category. Sometimes things work out like; I wanted to make sure I was getting as much cashback as possible. Still, at the same time, I was able to get credit lines as high as $16,000, but when you chase two categories, you make it impossible for you to maximize one. If you aren't maximizing these rewards, you are wasting your time.

Playing the game the right way.

Banks issuing credit cards often entice new possible card users with 0% introductory rates, 0% apr on balance transfers, and sign up bonuses. These all can be used to your advantage.

0 percent introductory rates range anywhere from 5-16 months and allow you to use the card interest-free for that time. As mentioned earlier in the book, introductory rates are what saved me from drowning in credit card debt and finance my first business. Because I was unable to get traditional loans because of my unstable income. I used three cards that had 0% introductory rates, one to pay down my debt, and the rest I used to fund my business, no interest paid on any of the money I borrowed. You may be asking yourself, "how does the credit card company make money then?" the credit card companies are in it for the long game and are banking on you going out on a shopping spree and overextending yourself. After you overextend yourself, the card issuer is banking on you, just forgetting about the high balance on the card. At the same time, you continue to make the minimum payment until the introductory rate period is up and boom those high-interest rates come back to bite you. If you want to avoid this, you can do the math, ask yourself how much money you use on the card then set yourself on a monthly payment that will allow you to pay down that balance before the introductory rate period is up.

I have friends who have taken advantage of business opportunities, travel at a discounted rate, and get money back on things they were already going to buy. Also, I have done two out of three myself, fund my business, and get cash back. I am supposed to believe you should never use your credit because some financial guru on youtube told me that credit and debt are wrong. Even though the gurus didn't get rich penny pinching and never using debt, the gurus got rich telling you not use debt in books, youtube videos, and radio shows. All debt is not bad debt; any debt that allows me to produce something rather than consume something is good debt.

Traveling for free or for little to nothing is quite possible with the correct information. Sign up bonuses that credit card issuers offer when you apply and get approved for a card will play a role in your journey if you have decided that you want to travel for free. This game is always changing, so you are going to keep yourself updated on a website like 'UScreditcard. com. I have no affiliation with the site; I just use it myself.

Most of these cards require you to spend in the thousands in the first few months to qualify for these signup bonuses. Spending requirements will range anywhere from $2,000 in spending in the first three months to $5,000. Most people have no reason to use any card for $5,000 in 3 months. Hence, they count themselves out and never even try to go for these rewards because if they spent $5,000 in the months for sign up bonus points, it would put them deep in a hole. Manufactured spending comes into play and allows those who are unable to spend $5,000 in a month.

Manufacturing spending is when you buy cash using your rewards credit card to meet spending requirements to receive rewards and get different bonuses. What works and what does not work changes continuously without fail. By the time you are reading this, what worked for someone else might not work for you, so I urge you to stay updated using websites like UScreditcardguide.com.

CHAPTER 14

Credit Card Sins

BEING APPROVED FOR new cards, getting high limits, and enjoying the benefits of having a strong credit score is exciting. In addition to this having a good score also gives you peace of mind; you won't have to worry about cutting corners when it comes to your credit. Here are some pitfalls to watch out for when you are on this journey.

Maxing out your card

Maxing out your credit card will significantly lower your credit score. Despite all the information on credit cards, people still believe that maxing out your card will not affect our score as long as you make the minimum payments. This just isn't the case, so make sure you are not maxing out your card.

Going over your credit limit

Just because your credit card issuer authorized a charge does not mean it won't affect your relationship with that card issuer. Good luck getting credit limit increases when you have gone over your limit. Having a balance higher than your limit can also happen when you max out a card and only pay the minimum payment. Interest begins to rack up, and it racks up quickly. You will be deemed irresponsible, and it will be tough getting credit limit increases going forward.

Opening a lot of new accounts to seem like you have high limits

If you open six accounts that all have $2,000 limits to make it seem as if you have a lot of available credit, it will not be a good look. You want to get your selected cards that align with your credit goals. Once you get the cards, get them to as high as limits as possible by seasoning the credit lines over time with on-time payments and low utilization. Opening a bunch of accounts to make it seems as if you have high limits, you will be marked an **impulsive borrower.**

Applying for too much credit at once

When it comes to applying for a lot of credit, you want to make sure you use your logic. You are not going to go and get four credit cards the day before you go out to shop for that new car you have had your eye on, it just Wouldn't make sense. Application sprees are fine as long as you have some sort of strategy attached to that application spree.

Taking out cash advances

Taking out cash advances is just never a good idea. So many different fees and interest usually starts accumulating soon as the money is taken out of the ATM. You can use the manufactured spending strategy we spoke about earlier in the book to liquidate your cards if you need to

Maximize your credit lines

There is a certain way you go about maximizing credit lines with each card issuer, and you must keep in mind this is the long game; you can't expect to walk before you crawl.

Stage one ($300-$1,000)

These are your starter line of credit; credit card issuers offer new users low limits to test the waters. Low utilization will demonstrate how responsible the new card user will be with the line of credit. It will give the card issuer an idea of what your financial habits look like, and this will determine if you will be granted higher limits. If you cannot handle a $500 credit card limit, then you definitely cannot handle a $5,000 limit. Be careful with these low limits; your utilization rate can rise easily. If you have a $500 limit and you carry a balance of $250, your utilization is 50%, and your score will take a hit.

Store cards such as Khols, Gap, Lowes, or Victoria secret, etc. are an option at this level, but I relying on these cards will not help you in the long run. A lot of store credit cards have fees and high-interest rates. Make sure your focus is getting cards from big banks such as Citi or American Express.

Stage two ($1,500-$4,000)

When you get to stage to you will begin to be surprised by how generous credit card issuers will be. When you are approved, and you will be in a position to ask your card issuer for limit increases. Your utilization and your ability to pay back high balances will be watched closely at this stage. If you have managed to get this far, you pay your bills on time and keep your utilization reasonably low. If you want to get to that next level, then you must keep your utilization anywhere from 1%-7%. Doing so will speed up the process and help you get to the next step faster. Great Cards that fall into this category

Stage three ($5,000-$10,000)

At this stage, you have a high score, and creditors are more than generous with you. Keeping your utilization low at this stage should be relatively easy, depending on how many cards you have. Getting to this level will be simple; you just make sure you periodically ask the creditors for increases. In my experience, I faced no financial scrutiny from credit card issuers. I never had to prove my income, never had to submit any tax information, so this shouldn't be a problem as long as you have a strong credit score.

Stage four ($11,000-$20,000)

Once you have gotten here you have built a great relationship with your banks, you have a solid score, and you have been responsible with the credit you have had access to up to this point. This stage is the promised land when it comes to consumer credit limits; some cards will grant you higher limits. If you need higher limits, building business credit is a much better option as a lot of your credit card limits for business will start at the $15,000-$20,000. Business credit will come into play because of the way the creditors see it; most consumers do not need such high limits. In contrast, businesses do need them.

Keep in mind...

Card issuers want to issue higher limits so because they make their money off of the interest paid by card users who carry balances. With American Express, you qualify for a 3x credit line increase after 61 days and qualify for another 3x increase after six months. I have taken all my starter credit cards with American express and have increased the limit to $12,000 on each one of them.

Getting six figures in Revolving credit

Almost anyone can reach six figures in revolving credit lines and have no proof of income, and they can get it in 24 months or less. I know this because I did it at 19. It only took me a year and a couple of months to achieve this goal of mine.` The rule here is that a closed mouth does not get fed. If you never ask for credit limit increases, chances are you won't get any. The only company that has given me a credit limit increase without me asking is American Express. Request limit increases whenever they are available. Yes, companies can provide you with increases without you asking, and it happens, but this is the exception, not the rule.

Dealing with denials

Earlier in the book, I talked a little bit about how to get over credit card denials here what you need to know when it comes to denials. Watch out for the Chase 5 in 24 rule, if you have five recently opened accounts in the past 24 months you will automatically be denied. I do not have any chase cards. I prefer Citi and Amex, but if a Chase Card is on your radar, be aware of that.

If and when you go to apply for more than one card in a day, there is a chance that you may be denied. Denials can happen for many different reasons. It can be because you have a thin credit file or due to high amounts of debt in that case return to the eliminate credit card debt section before you do any of this. If you do end up getting denied or not getting instant approval, you can call the **reconsideration line**. When you call the reconsideration line, the card issuer lets you plead your case as to why you should be approved and also goes over why you were denied. Most of the time, the individuals that work for the card issuers deal with angry people all day long, be as pleasant as you can, and try to make a friend. In some instances, you get someone who is very rude, dismissive, and does not care to help you. In this case, you hang up and call again to increase your chances of getting someone more pleasant and who is more willing to help on the phone. Keep in mind the person on the phone has the power of granting you a credit line; they do not get a pay cut if you get approved. With that said, if you can get into some kind of rapport with the person on the phone, you increase your chances of them approving you and, if not, hang up and call again. The most I have hung up and called again is six times for my more high-end cards, but I know people who have called 20 times, but how much you call is ultimately up to you as there is no 'sweet spot.'

"Show me an 800 credit score, and I will show you someone who understands credit"

CHAPTER 15

Getting a score of 800+

IF YOUR GOAL is to get the highest score possible, I am going to give you the exact formula for an 800+ credit score. Apply these strategies will almost guarantee you a score of 800+ unless there is some considerable algorithm change. Apply these ten principals and watch you score skyrocket

> **Keep your utilization between 1%-7%**
> **No late payments in the past seven years**
> **Have 3 to 6 open credit cards with high limits**
> **No collections for the past seven-year**
> **No bankruptcies, foreclosures or tax liens for the past ten years**
> **No Hard money loans on record**
> **Accounts have been opened and established for well over five years**
> **Have two addresses reporting on your credit file to show stability**
> **Have you installment loans reporting paid as agreed**
> **NO COSIGNING**

I know a lot of this seems repetitive. Like I am beating it over your head, but consider this, you are bombarded with advertising, images, and music that promotes reckless spending poor financial habits and irresponsibility. This behavior gets normalized with the help of cute little sayings like "Yolo" or "I work hard I deserve it," "Shop til you drop," and an infinite amount of sayings that the media hits you with via television, social media, and music. One thing that is crucial to fixing credit and creating financial prosperity is understanding that the images you are sold on tv, and social media of shopping sprees, fleets of exotic cars, and excessive consumerism isn't wealth. It may seem as if those things mentioned are what create wealth, but in reality, they destroy it. You will never get rich maxing out a credit card at Louis Vuitton and posting it on Instagram. Who does get rich, Louis Vuitton, and the credit card company. Don't get me wrong here, I am all for a life of luxury, but If your goal is to prosper financially, mortgaging your future for a one-day shopping won't do it.

I am not going to sit here and tell you exactly how to run or manage your finances. Still, I am going to sit here and inform you of all the traps that are set up to make it harder for you to get ahead, and that will keep you living paycheck to paycheck.

"Knowledge without application is useless."

CHAPTER 16

Final Thoughts

IF YOU HAVE gotten to this part in the book, I thank you for your time spent. I also thank you for trusting me to get you the truth about improving your credit to achieve homeownership.

Before you conclude whether or not the information I have given you will work or not, I urge you to take bits and pieces of this information and live by it for a while and experience its results. Many people spend their days watching finance gurus on YouTube but never do anything to change. Let me be clear here while this book has equipped you with the information you need to win the game; reading this does not mean you're winning. You do not win until you go out there and play the game and apply the knowledge. Knowledge means nothing without application of it. Do not let this be another book you read and think, "oh, that's good stuff," only never to use a single thing I said in this book. Return to this book frequently and let it act as your credit guide.

My commitment to you, my clients, and anyone else who consumes my content is to help them achieve a level of financial literacy. The more individuals we can help become financially literate, the less these corporations can profit from ignorance. If you got value out of this book, share it with a friend or family member. I enjoyed writing this and sharing this information with you; I hope you enjoyed our time together. We'll talk soon!

DISPUTE LETTER SECTION

1st Round Letters

Vernell Watts
123 ABC Street
000-00-0000
Bureau_address
Current Date

To Whom It May Concern,

This letter is a formal complaint that you are reporting inaccurate and incomplete credit information on my Credit Report.

I understand that mistakes happen but your inaccurate information could cost me in higher interest rates and I have enough expenses as it is. Please investigate the following information and either remove it or at least send me the information that you used to add it to my report.

(Dispute Explanation)

Sincerely yours,

SIGNATURE

Round 2

John Smith
123 Abc street
01/02/1990
123-45-6789
Bureau Address

Customer Relations Department

Current date

To Whom It May Concern:

I am concerned about the validity and accuracy of your recent investigation of these accounts that are reporting on my credit report. 30 days ago I requested an investigation because I felt the item(s) below were not being reported accurately and legally. A few days ago I received a letter stating your investigation was complete. Please explain to me how you conducted your investigation!

1. Please explain to me what your representatives uncovered to lead them to believe that you are reporting this item as it legally should be reported?
2. What certified documents were reviewed to conclude your investigation?
3. Please provide a complete copy of all of the information that was transmitted to the data furnisher as part of the investigation.

4. What did it cost your company to obtain the documents required to complete your investigation?
5. Please provide proof of your timely procurement of certified documents.
6. Did you speak directly to any agent of the company that was reporting the information to confirm the accuracy of what you are reporting?
7. If yes to above:
   a. Who did you speak to?
   b. On what date?
   c. How long was the conversation?
   d. What was their position?
   e. What telephone number did you call?
   f. What is the name of the employee of your company that spoke directly to the above party?
   g. What is the position of the employee of your company that spoke directly to the above party?
   h. How long has that employee been employed at your company?
   i. What formal training was provided to this employee to investigate items of this kind?
   j. Was there any email or written communication between members of your company and the above party?

8. If so, please provide copies of all correspondence; supply copies of any and all conclusive documentation to prove that you have in fact conducted a reasonable investigation of the account in question.
9. Provide the date of the commencement of delinquency
10. Provide the SPECIFIC date reporting that these items will cease

Enclosed with your response to the above questions I respectfully request a notarized affidavit confirming the information that is provided is true and correct as per my civil rights granted under several federal laws. This information should not come as a form letter response.

My initial dispute was detailed and directly related to the account in question. A template response will not be an acceptable response. If you cannot supply ALL of the above information in a timely manner as detailed in several laws, including but not limited to the Fair Credit Reporting Act, I must immediately demand the permanent removal of this item from my credit report.

This erroneous entry is detrimental to my overall credit rating and has caused me severe financial and emotional distress. If you choose not to provide the above-requested deletion or requested/required documentation of your investigation, I will pursue the enforcement of my constitutional rights via federal court proceedings. As you are well aware this information will come out through my formal discovery process and necessary depositions. I have recently studied constitutional consumer protection laws along with civil/federal court procedures. I will represent myself pro-se and will formally request a jury trial.

Please respond accordingly,

Signature

_____

Round 3 letter

Vernell Watts
123 ABC Street

Transunion
P.O. Box 2000
Chester, PA 19016-2000

RE: American Express Credit Card

To whom it may concern,

I have Obtained my credit report, and I have noticed several errors on the account

I have never been 90 days late; please remove this.

This is being reported as an open account; please remove this.

No payment was made in 5/2010

The date of the first delinquency with original creditors is not provided, please provide this
The card limit is reporting as $3,000 which is incorrect; please correct this

Please correct or remove this information as this incorrect information is damaging my financial situation and causing great financial distress. Please respond within the legal time frame stated in the FCRA. A template response will not be an acceptable response. I await your response.

Signature

_____

Personal Information

Vernell Watts
123 ABC Street
01/01/1990
000-00-0000

CREDIT BUREAUS ADDRESS

CURRENT DATE

To Whom It May Concern,

This letter is a formal complaint that you are reporting inaccurate and incomplete credit information on my credit report.

I understand that mistakes happen, but your inaccurate information could hurt me in the future and cost me a job, dream house, car or force me to pay higher interest rates and I have enough stress as it is.

Please remove any names, addresses, and employers listed on my credit profile that are not the following:

YOUR NAME
YOUR CURRENT ADDRESS
YOUR CURRENT EMPLOYER

I've included proof of my name and address with this letter.

Thank you in advance for correcting this information! I would also like a credit report from you to verify the changes once you're done updating my file.

Thank You,

Signature

_____

Kevin David
2232 Apple Cove St
Beverly Hills CA
Phone: 760-792-5643

(Bureau Address)

To Whom it may concern,

I recently received a copy of my credit report and noticed some addresses that do not belong to me or have be obsolete for quite some time. For the safety and accurate reporting of my information, I request that the following obsolete addresses be removed from my credit report immediately;

2234 Apple Wine St Las Vegas NV 89118

3765 Gentle Breeze St Las Vegas NV 89168

2347 Red Rock Cove Las Vegas NV 89165

I have provided a copy of my identification card and my social security card to verify my identity and current address. Please notify any creditors who may be reporting any unauthorized past accounts that are connected with these mentioned addresses as I have exhausted all of my options with the furnishers.

Once the information is updated please send a copy of my updated credit report to the address above.

Signature

_____

No Response Letters

No response for 30 days

Adam Smith
123 ABC Street
12/09/1979
000-00-0000
Bureau Address
Date

To Whom It May Concern,

This letter shall serve as formal notice of my intent to file a complaint with the FTC, due to your blatant and objectionable disregard of the law.

As indicated by the attached copies of letters and mailing receipts, you have received and accepted through registered mail my dispute letter dated, as well as my follow-up letter dated. To date, you have not done your duty as mandated by law. Your non-compliance with federal law is unacceptable, your disregard for it contemptible. Rest

Federal law requires you to respond within 30 days, yet you have failed to respond. Failure to comply with these federal regulations by credit reporting agencies are investigated by the Federal Trade Commission (see 15 USC 41, et seq.).

I am maintaining a careful record of my communications with you on this matter; for the purpose of filing a complaint with the FTC. If you continue in your non-compliance. I further remind you that, as in Wenger v. Trans Union Corp., No. 95-6445 (C.D.Cal. Nov. 14, 1995), you may be liable for your willful noncompliance.

For the record, the following information is being erroneously included on my credit report, as I have advised you on two separate occasions, more than 75 days and again 40 days ago:

Mention account disputed

If you do not immediately remove this inaccurate and incomplete information, I will file a formal complaint with the Federal Trade Commission.

Under federal law, you had 30 days to complete your re-investigation, yet you have failed to respond. Further delays are inexcusable.

Be advised that the description of the procedure used to determine the accuracy and completeness of the information is at this moment requested as well, to be provided within 15 days of the completion of your re-investigation.

Sincerely,

Signature

No response for 60 Days

Vernell Watts
1234 ABC Street
12/14/1996
000-00-0000
Bureau Address
Date

To Whom It May Concern,

This letter is formal notice that you have failed to respond promptly to my dispute letter of insert date, deposited by registered mail with the U.S. Postal Service on that date. Federal law requires you to respond within thirty (30) days, yet you have failed to respond. Failure to comply with these federal regulations by credit reporting agencies are investigated by the Federal Trade Commission (FTC) (see 15 USC 41, et seq.).

I am maintaining a careful record of my communications with you for the purpose of filing a complaint with the FTC should you continue in your non-compliance. I further remind you that, as in Wenger v. Trans Union Corp., No. 95-6445 (C.D.Cal. Nov. 14, 1995), you may be liable for your willful non-compliance.

Be aware that I am making a final goodwill attempt to have you clear up this matter. You have 15 days to cure.

For your benefit, and as a gesture of my goodwill, I will restate my dispute. The following information needs to be verified and, following failure to verify, deleted from the report as soon as possible:

(Mention items disputed)

The listed item is entirely inaccurate and incomplete and represents a very serious error in your reporting. Please delete this misleading information and supply a corrected credit profile to all creditors who have received a copy within the last six months, or the last two years for employment purposes.

Additionally, please provide the name, address, and telephone number of each credit grantor or other subscribers.

Under federal law, you had thirty (30) days to complete your re-investigation, yet you have failed to respond. Do not delay any further.

Be advised that the description of the procedure used to determine the accuracy and completeness of the information is as a result of this request as well, to be provided within fifteen (15) days of the completion of your re-investigation.

Sincerely yours,

Signature

Inquiry Removal Letter

Vernell Watts
1234 ABC Street
Bureau Address
Current Date

RE: Request for Investigation of Unauthorized Inquiry

To Whom It May Concern,

I checked my personal credit report, which I received from your organization, and I noticed that these unauthorized inquiries have been made:

(List of inquiries)

I contacted the creditors who have placed these inquiries and asked them to remove them from my credit report. I also asked them to cease their illegal activities immediately, but to date, there have been no responses from their side. Since sending the letter more than 30 business days ago, they have failed to respond and honor my request.

I request your help in resolving this matter. In accordance with the Fair Credit Reporting Act, I request you immediately initiate an investigation into this inquiry on my credit report to determine who authorized the inquiry. If, once your investigation is complete, you find my allegation to be true, please remove the unauthorized inquiry from my credit report and send me an updated copy of my credit report at my address listed above.

If you do find the inquiry referenced above to be valid, I request that you please send me a full description of the procedures used in your investigation within 15 business days of the completion of the investigation.

Thank you for your help.

Sincerely,

Signature

_____

Kevin David
2232 Apple Cove St
Beverly Hills CA
Phone: 760-792-5643

(Bureau Address)

To whom it may concern,

I checked my credit reports and found some inquiries from companies that I did not allow to access my credit reports. I am concerned about all of the activity going on with all of my credit reports. I demand the removal of these inquiries to avoid any confusion because I did not initiate these inquires or give consent electronically, in person or over the phone. I am aware that without permissible purpose no entity can pull my credit unless otherwise noted in section 604 of the FCRA.

The following companies did not have permission to request my credit report:

1. Toyota Motor Credit on 07/05/2019
2. Lexus Motor Credit on 07/06/2019
3. Bankcorp Credit Union 06/08/2018
4. Chase INC on 05/07/2019

Again, I demand the removal of these unauthorized inquiries immediately.

Please send me an updated copy of my credit report to the

above address. According to the FCRA, there shall be no charge for this update report. Thank you

Signature

_____

3rd Party Credit Bureau Letters

Adam Smith
1234 ABC Street
Las Vegas Nevada
Birthday: 02/07/1996
SSN: 000-00-0000

Sage Stream LLC

I wish to freeze my credit report with your company. Please Acknowledge my request with a prompt response. Thank you,

Signature

_____

Ashley Costella
4567 Apple Cove St
Beverly Hills CA 76254
03/06/2018
SSN: 000-00-0000
ChexSystems
Attn: Consumer Relations
7805 Hudson Road, Suite 100
Woodbury, MN 55125

To Whom It May Concern,

I recently received a copy of my ChexSystems record, and I have found several inaccuracies in the report.

{dispute_item_and_explanation}

In detail, you recorded that I had non-sufficient funds with [name of bank] on or around [date]. I am disputing this record because I believe it to be inaccurate. Please request evidence of this unresolved outstanding negative record from [bank name] and investigate this item for me.

I understand that your repository is required by law to begin an investigation for me because you are a credit-reporting agency and must follow the Fair Credit Reporting Act. I await your results.

Kind regards,

Signature

_____

Pay for a Deletion Letter

Jessica Sanchez
6757 mineral st
Las Vegas NV 877654

Creditor Name
Creditor Address
Creditor phone #

Date

Dear Collection Manager:

It has come to my attention, through my credit report, there is a claim I owe a debt to your company. I can save us both some effort and time by settling the debt.

Below reads my offer. This is not a renewed promise to pay, nor does it constitute any agreement unless you sign and returned to me at the address listed above.

Please Note that I have not yet agreed that this debt is mine and I still reserve the right to seek additional proof of this debt from your company.

Because you hold all the rights to report the debt to the credit bureaus as you see fit, you can certainly change that listing at any time as the source reporting the debt.

I do not doubt that you are aware of my right to dispute this debt and request full proof of my obligation to the debt. Paying this unverified debt to you has no value to me if we cannot mutually agree that you will report the debt as outlined below.

While I realize that your function is to collect debts as a collections agency, I am also aware that a paid collection would not be favorable on my report. With that being said, I have determined, through the bureaus, that you have the absolute right to report this debt as you see fit or not report it at all.

If you indicate that you are unable to remove the negative listing on my credit report, I will be forced to cease communication and request verification of the debt.

My goal is to arrange a term that is acceptable to us both since this debt is "questionable."

My Offer: I will pay your company the amount of $__ as "payment in full for the full satisfaction of this account." Upon receipt of the above payment, your company will agree to change this entry on my credit reports to "Paid" immediately. You further agree to remove any and all previous delinquencies.

If you approve and agree to these terms, please acknowledge with your signature and return this letter to me. You agree these terms herein are confidential and that you have the authority to make such decisions. No payment will be made without written confirmation.

Upon receipt of this signed acknowledgment, I will immediately mail you funds by priority mail. This is not a renewed promise to pay but rather a restricted offer only. If no terms can be met, no new arrangements will be made, and the offer will be withdrawn.

_____

Signature of company officer

_____

Print Company Officer name
Date:

Sincerely,

Frivolous Dispute Response

Jared Jhonson
3456 Fairfax Ave
Hollywood CA 89156
000-00-0000
Bureau Address
Date

To Whom It May Concern,

I received a letter from your firm stating that my letter is requesting verification of erroneous items on my report as being classified as "frivolous" or "irrelevant." I assure you that in no way do I consider a matter of such importance to me as frivolous or irrelevant. If you do not honor my original request to verify the items in my previous letter, mailed (DATE SENT) via certified mail, I will file a complaint with the Federal Trade Commission against your company.

I have included my original disputes for your convenience below:

The following information, therefore, needs to be reinvestigated. I respectfully request to be provided proof of this alleged item, specifically the contract, note or other instrument bearing my signature. Failing that, the items must be deleted from the report as soon as possible:

(Dispute Explanation)

The listed item is completely inaccurate and incomplete and is a very serious error in reporting. Please delete this misleading information, and supply a corrected credit profile to all creditors who have received a copy within the last six months, or the last two years for employment purposes.
Additionally, please provide the name, address, and telephone number of each credit grantor or other subscribers.

Under federal law, you have 30 days to complete your reinvestigation. Be advised that the description of the procedure used to determine the accuracy and completeness of the information is at this moment requested as well. Please provide this information within 15 days of the completion of your re-investigation.

Sincerely yours,

Signature

Reinsertion Dispute

Jessica Sanchez
6757 mineral st
Las Vegas NV 877654

To whom it may concern

I am requesting immediate removal of an inaccurate item that has been reinserted on to my credit report.

(Account number) I recently reviewed a copy of past and current credit reports and I found that your company has allowed an inaccurate item to be reinserted on to my credit report after it has been deleted.

According to the FCRA I have a right to be provided with the proper documents and certification required to for reinsertion of this account. I would like to be provided with copies of those documents and certifications.

Under FCRA section 611 (a)(5)(ii) "reinserted in the file the consumer reporting agency shall notify the consumer of the reinsertion in writing not later than 5 business days after the reinsertion, or if authorized by the consumer for that purpose, by any other means available to the agency.

(iii) Additional information. As a part of or in addition to the notice under clause (ii), a consumer reporting agency shall provide to a consumer in writing not later than 5 business days after the date of the reinsertion.

I have yet to be notified. I am disputing this item. I will allow your company a 15 day period to furnish this information. However, if you do not provide the information requested you must delete this account as required by the FCRA. Please send an update copy of my credit report once my request has been completed.

Signature

_____

CPSIA information can be obtained
at www.ICGtesting.com
Printed in the USA
JSHW030214230222
23217JS00007B/218